# RAILROADS TO SUPERHIGHWAYS

## A Handbook on Big Ideas
## That Have Made Our World Smaller

### Hwee Goh
### Illustrated by David Liew

**Marshall Cavendish** Children

ISBN 978-981-49-2821-2 (Hardcover Edition)
ISBN 978-981-5066-00-5 (Paperback Edition)

Published by Marshall Cavendish Children
An imprint of Marshall Cavendish International

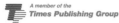
A member of the
**Times Publishing Group**

Other Marshall Cavendish Offices:
Marshall Cavendish Corporation, 800 Westchester Ave, Suite N-641, Rye
Brook, NY 10573, USA • Marshall Cavendish International (Thailand) Co Ltd,
253 Asoke, 16th Flr, Sukhumvit 21 Road, Klongtoey Nua, Wattana, Bangkok
10110, Thailand • Marshall Cavendish (Malaysia) Sdn Bhd, Times Subang,
Lot 46, Subang Hi-Tech Industrial Park, Batu Tiga, 40000 Shah Alam,
Selangor Darul Ehsan, Malaysia

Marshall Cavendish is a registered trademark of Times Publishing Limited

**National Library Board, Singapore Cataloguing in Publication Data**

Names: Goh, Hwee. | Liew, David, illustrator.
Title: Railroads to superhighways : a handbook on big ideas that have made
our world smaller / Hwee Goh ; illustrated by David Liew.
Other title(s): Change makers.
Description: Singapore : Marshall Cavendish Children, [2020]
Identifiers: OCN 1201649056 | ISBN 978-981-49-2821-2 (hardcover) |
978-981-5066-00-5 (paperback)
Subjects: LCSH: Inventions--History--Juvenile literature. | Technological
innovations--History--Juvenile literature.
Classification: DDC 609--dc23

Printed in Singapore

# CONTENTS

# REVOLUTION BY RAILROAD

The arrival of the railroad in the early 19th century **changes the game** on how people connect all over the world. It brings about a 'quicker' time, a 'shorter' distance and the ability to break new frontiers.

**What's That?**
To **change the game** is to do something differently and change things for the better.

**Did You Know?**
The exact same thing has been said of the Internet.

**Did You Know?**
The notion of 'impatience' is also said to have developed at this time!

## Get with the Groove

As early as 600 BC, the Greeks cut grooves into limestone roads, building a 'railway' to move wheeled carts along. However, this disappeared when the Romans conquered the Greeks a few hundred years later.

### Did You Know?
The wheel is said to have been invented around 3500 BC for pottery. About 300 years later, the wheel is put on a chariot, and the rest is history!

I THOUGHT GETTING CIVILISED MEANT THINGS WERE SUPPOSED TO **PROGRESS**??

GREEK ROAD

NOW UNDER ROMAN MANAGEMENT

### Did You Know?
In the late 1800s, Singapore had tramways that ran across the island. It was 10 cents for first class seats and six cents for second class seats — too expensive even for those who enjoyed hand-pulled rickshaws!

## Horse in front of the Cart

It wasn't till the early 1550s that the Germans put wooden rails on dirt roads to make it easier for horses to pull wagons through. These became 'tramways', which were later powered by steam or electricity.

5

## A Puffing Devil!

A major game changer comes in the early 1800s. Englishman Samuel Homfray makes a bet that he could carry 10 tons of iron and 70 men on a tramway with steam power. This first ever steam locomotive (and five extra wagons) takes hours to travel 14.5 km (9 mi) through Wales.

### Did You Know?

Richard Trevithick is the man Homfray hires to build this 'iron horse'. Before this, there were no self-running vehicles ever. Sadly, Trevithick's genius is not recognised, and he is buried in a pauper's grave in 1833.

NOT ALL OF HERO'S EXPERIMENTS WORKED ...

HERO THE INVENTOR →

KA-BOOM!

I guess home insurance hasn't been invented yet, has it?

HERO THE SANDWICH *

* not invented till the 1930s

### Did You Know?

An early steam-powered engine was invented in 1712 by Englishman Thomas Newcomen to pump water out of coal mines, a job usually done using horses.

### What's That?

A **nozzle** is a round spout at the end of a pipe.

## Powered by Water

Early in the 1st century, a Greek man named Hero boiled water and expelled the steam through a **nozzle** — discovering steam power! Centuries later in 1825, steam powers the first passenger train called Locomotion, built by Englishman George Stephenson.

## Watt is the Answer

Where did all the water in a steam engine go? It went back into the boiler to be reheated, wasting energy. Scottish engineer James **Watt** creates a separate condenser for this cooled water, making the steam power more efficient, and reducing the use of coal (to boil the water) by two-thirds.

## From One Revolution to Another

The steam engine is credited for powering the Industrial Revolution, which transformed Britain and then Europe and the US.

- Factories used to be built around waterways, so that raw materials and goods could be transported up- and downstream. Trains and steam boats enabled this to be done faster, and into inland areas.

- Machines used to be powered by humans, animals or the wind. Now they ran much faster, on steam power.

## General Standard Train Time

Before the railroad, the concept of time depended on when the sun came up and went down wherever you lived. It was simply a local matter — what time you went to the grocers, and what time you delivered goods on horse cart.

### What's That?
The **Greenwich Mean Time (GMT)** is measured at noon when the sun is at the highest point on the prime meridian, which sits at longitude 0 in Greenwich, UK.

The railroad forces the need for a standard time across the train route. In Britain, the Great Western Railway adopts **Greenwich Mean Time (GMT)** in 1840.

### Did You Know?
There is a small time zone that exists only at the Queen's homes in Windsor Castle and Buckingham Palace in the UK.
All the clocks are set 5 minutes faster, so that the food arrives on time!

# CAMELS AND CARAVANS

Between 130 BC and 1453, the Silk Road is a major 6,400 km (4,000 mi) east-west network connecting China through the Middle East to Europe.
On these routes, there are trading posts and busy markets. Goods are bought and sold many times along the way, until they reach the other end.

### Silk Seres Seres

Despite being two empires set so far apart in the 2nd century BC, the Chinese and the Romans both love silk. In both societies, the status of an individual is reflected in the silk they wear. In fact, the ancient Roman word for China is "Seres", meaning the "land of silk".

## The World's First Trade Secret

The Romans thought silk grew on trees (well, the silkworm larvae did!) while the Chinese held on tightly to their secrets of silkworm farming.

Around the year 550, the Roman Emperor Justinian sends two monks to Asia and they return with silkworm eggs hidden inside their walking sticks, finally bringing the silk industry to Europe.

### Did You Know?
The earliest evidence of the silk trade from China was found on an Egyptian mummy (wearing silk) from 1070 BC.

### What's That?
This becomes the first known case of industrial **espionage** (es-spear-nahj): the theft of trade secrets from a competitor.

# The Great Han Export

The Silk Road is formally opened by the Chinese in 130 BC. This trade route brings two major inventions to the rest of the world:

- Paper. Invented in China during the 2nd century, the use of paper spread through the Silk Road to Samarkand (now in Uzbekistan) in 700 and gradually moved to Europe.

- Gunpowder. There have been references to fireworks and firearms in China as early as the 900s, and historians believe gunpowder was exported to Europe in the 1200s. This was a major game changer for Europe because it gave power to nations at war.

## A Crucible for Cultures

Everything is up for exchange between the two regions: fruits, vegetables, grain, metals and more importantly, science,

**Did You Know?**
A crucible is a container, brought to high temperatures to make something new.

language and culture. Unfortunately, the plague also travels along the Silk Road in both directions, and possibly brings the Black Death to Europe.

Why do I have to carry the creepy guy?

Who's the guy in black?

No idea. Doesn't talk much... Only wants to get to Rome from Xian.

Oh, we're starting on THAT again are we? So how long before we mice (acting as rats) get blamed for EVERYTHING?*

*See Change Makers: Invisible Enemies

## A Train of Camels

A camel caravan is a string of camels carrying passengers and goods. This is perfect for the harsh conditions of the Silk Road, especially because camels can go a week without water and months without food. When they do stop to drink, they can gulp up to

**Did You Know?**
Camels are used to carry vaccines in solar-powered refrigerators to remote areas of the Sahara.

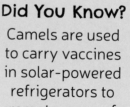

100 litres (26.5 gal) of water in 10 minutes. Camels can also carry very heavy loads over long distances.

## Marco Polo by Camel

Together with his father and uncle, Venetian teenage explorer Marco Polo travels on the Silk Road from Italy to China in the 1270s. He is said to have lived there for 17 years, becoming an **emissary** for Mongolian leader Kublai Khan and returning to Venice only in his 40s. When *The Travels of Marco Polo* is published, readers believe it to be a work of fiction. Only after his death does the world realise these tales might just be true.

### What's That?

As an **emissary**, Polo represented the Khan in various parts of the Mongol Empire, speaking many languages and perhaps collecting taxes.

### Did You Know?

Historians believe that when Columbus landed, he thought he was on the Asian continent, off the Indian Ocean. This was how the Native Indians (actually in the Americas) were so named.

## This Ain't China?

Polo's travels, based on stories he told Italian writer, Rustichello, were written and reproduced by hand. They became the definitive account of the people, culture and knowledge of the East. Inspired by this centuries later, another Italian, Christopher Columbus, famously goes looking for China by sea, but instead lands on what is now the Bahamas.

SILK ROAD
TRANSPORTATION

*From Beijing to London*

OCEAN ROADS
FREIGHT

CARAVANSERAI

EAST TO WEST
AND BACK AGAIN

**Did You Know?**
Caravanserai were courtyard inns that sprouted along the Silk Road, built like fortresses to keep travellers (and their precious cargo) safe from bandits.

## The 21st Century Silk Road

Towards the end of 2013, Chinese President Xi Jinping calls for a multibillion-dollar Belt and Road Initiative. It is also known as the New Silk Road or 一带一路 (yí dài yí lù), One Belt, One Road:

- One Belt will connect China's inner lands through the old Silk Road to Central Asia and Europe.

- One Road will connect by sea, southeastern China through South East Asia to the Middle East and Europe.

China's strategy is to extend its economic capacity to its smaller neighbours, but this has also been perceived as a political plan to build its empire and influence.

# HOT OFF THE PRESS

The invention of the printing press in Europe in the 1450s changes the course of history forever — making everything possible from the spread of science and news, down to your school textbooks today. Before this, books and literacy were only for an elite few who could afford a hand-copied book.

## The Diamond Sutra

In the year 868, a Chinese man has a woodblock engraved, to print a 5-m (17-ft) long Buddhist scroll translated from **Sanskrit**. At the bottom of it, he inscribes, "Made for universal free distribution by Wang Jie on behalf of his parents." This scroll is now held in fairly good condition at the British Library, and is the oldest known printed book!

### What's That?
**Sanskrit** is one of the world's oldest languages and no longer spoken.

## Secret Library

The Diamond Sutra is first discovered in 1900, in the Caves of a Thousand Buddhas along the Silk Road in Dunhuang, northwest China. The caves contained thousands of ancient scrolls, and had been sealed off from invaders around the year 1000.

# Chip off the Block

As the Chinese refine the use of paper and ink, woodblock printing takes off in the 7th century. Chinese characters are carved in reverse on a piece of wood, inked and stamped to 'print' copies. In the next few centuries, this method passes on to Japan and Korea.

## Movable Type

In the 1040s, a Chinese man named Bi Sheng makes single Chinese characters from clay and lays them out on an iron plate. This is the first step towards the printing press, with reusable pieces which can be rearranged to print different texts. The Koreans take this further in the 13th century by printing with bronze movable type.

### Did You Know?

The art of block printing does not reach Europe as fast as paper does. But when movable type arrives in the 15th century, it is perfect for the Roman alphabet and a major change maker to printing.

# ODD BiTS O' HiSTORY...

## From Scrolls to the Codex

The book, as we know it, is a form of codex
with pages bound together under a cover.
The codex has taken over scrolls in the western world
by the 6th century, but does not catch on in China
until 300 years later. Being able to flip to a page
you needed on a codex was far superior to
unrolling a scroll until you found it.

## It All Comes Together

After years of experimenting, German goldsmith Johannes Gutenberg takes out a loan from his neighbour and starts the world's first printing press.

- Gutenberg is the first in Europe to use metal instead of wood letters.

- He creates reversed letters in brass and fits them tightly on a plate.

- He makes his own ink (which needs to stick on metal) and uses two large ink balls covered in goose skin to coat the letters.

- Finally, he adapts his 'press' from wine and olive oil presses. The paper is fixed on a board and the ink is pressed down using a screw to produce a clean print.

## The Gutenberg Bible

Gutenberg's printing press makes the production of books much cheaper and faster. His first major project is the production of the Bible in two volumes, before this, painstakingly hand-copied (and not always accurately). He prints 180 Bibles, which take three years to produce. About 20 intact copies survive to this day.

## No Press Without Paper

The printing press also makes the use of paper much more common. A Bible printed on parchment required the skin of 250 (dead!) sheep. With pamphlets and books now in the common people's hands, the rise of literacy feeds back to the rise of printing.

## Hefty Price Tag

At the time it was printed, it was believed
the Gutenberg Bible was pre-ordered and cost
30 guilder, about three years' wages of a clerk,
but much cheaper than a hand-copied book!
Experts now estimate that an intact copy could fetch
a princely US$35 million or more at an auction.

## A Book to Kill

In 1969, a man hides in the restroom of
Harvard University's library after the building closes
and steals two prized volumes of the Gutenberg Bible.
As he tries to climb back down a rope, he struggles with
the 30-kg (70-lb) weight and falls six storeys down.
He is found the next morning with a fractured skull.

.-/... .. - -. -./.. -. - - - .-./
-.-.... .- - -. - -. . *

Before the 19th century, information travels
only as fast (or as slow) as the rider on horseback.
While the printing press brings the world leaps forward
with news, pamphlets and books, these still
take days or even months to be delivered.

The Mongols had relays of riders
on fast horses to pass information
around their vast empire.

The Inca Empire had a similar
relay system, except that the messages
were passed on by RUNNERS ON FOOT.

Oh, the letter my cousin sent me
a YEAR ago just arrived!
"The barbarians are coming SOON. RUN!"

Hmm, I want to send a
postcard to my wife...
but I'm sure it'll get
there only AFTER
I reach home...

Oops... I left the
laundry hanging
on the line...

*Can you decipher the
title of this chapter? Read
on to find the answer!

In April 1775 in Boston, American Paul Revere needs to deliver a message to his fellow patriots that British troops are arriving. In case he is captured, he arranges for another man to hang lanterns from the town's bell tower — one lantern if the enemies are coming by land, two if by sea (actually the Charles River). The next day, the **American Revolution** starts.

## What's That?

The **American Revolution** (1775–1783) is the war that sees 13 American colonies win their independence from Britain. The colonies become a new country — the US.

## Did You Know?

You can read all about this "midnight ride" in *Paul Revere's Ride* by American poet Henry Wadsworth Longfellow.

## Smoke...

In ancient China, smoke signals were used to warn others further down the Great Wall of China, of incoming invaders. At the other end of the world, the Greeks used pairs of flame torches to signal letters of their alphabet.

## ...and Mirrors

The simple mirror is still highly recommended for survival kits. In the 1980s, a man on a rafting trip in the US is severely injured and owes his life to a signal mirror (and the SOS in Morse code) that is spotted from a jet plane more than 10,000 m (35,000 ft) in the sky.

### Did You Know?

The Chinese idiom 狼烟四起 (láng yān sì qǐ) — the smoke of the wolf rises — is used to describe impending war, and comes from smoke signal fires built using dried wolf dung.

Why is there SO MUCH SMOKE???

I can't see a thing!

Heh sorry... I sort of lost control of the signal fires...

## Fair Weather Friend

During the French Revolution in the 1790s, Frenchman Claude Chappe builds a series of hilltop stations across France. Messages from the war front are relayed from one station to the next using black and white panels to signal letters and numbers. There is also a telescope to read messages from other stations. Chappe calls it a *télégraphe* or "far writer", and it is widely adopted in Europe.

**What's That?**
These visual signals are called semaphore, which rely on a line of sight to work.

Monsieur Chappe, have you considered using black and white panels instead? It'll probably save a lot on the supply of bamboo leaves...

## Dashes and Dots

In the 1830s, American Samuel Morse develops a code to transmit messages quickly over long distances, using electrical signals on wires. At first, the long and short beeps are received as dashes and dots on paper. Telegraph operators catch on quickly and are able to just listen to the coded message and write it down.

### Morse Code Table

| | | | | | | | |
|---|---|---|---|---|---|---|---|
| A | ·− | N | −· | 0 | −−−−− | | |
| B | −··· | O | −−− | 1 | ·−−−− | | |
| C | −·−· | P | ·−−· | 2 | ··−−− | | |
| D | −·· | Q | −−·− | 3 | ···−− | | |
| E | · | R | ·−· | 4 | ····− | | |
| F | ··−· | S | ··· | 5 | ····· | | |
| G | −−· | T | − | 6 | −···· | | |
| H | ···· | U | ··− | 7 | −−··· | | |
| I | ·· | V | ···− | 8 | −−−·· | | |
| J | ·−−− | W | ·−− | 9 | −−−−· | | |
| K | −·− | X | −··− | . | ·−·−·− | | |
| L | ·−·· | Y | −·−− | , | −−·−− | | |
| M | −− | Z | −−·· | ? | ··−−·· | | |

## More Evolutionary than Revolutionary

As with the world's revolutionary ideas, the arrival of the electric telegraph is possible only because of trailblazers before Morse. These discoveries make the Morse telegraph possible:

- Electricity
- 'Batteries' to store electric currents
- Electromagnetism (that electricity creates a magnetic force that could move a needle or marker)

**Did You Know?**
Separately in Britain, a team develops a telegraph using magnetic needles that point to letters and numbers. The Morse system turns out to be easier to use worldwide.

Missed Moments in History...

Nice idea Oogblok, but you'll have to wait until the discovery of electricity before we can test it out....

Awww...

Shall I tell them about fire and suggest they start with smoke signals first?

Are you crazy? Did you see what happened on pages 24 and 25???

## Trains and Telegraphs

Telegraph wires were best laid along
the railroads, which already had the
right of way to pass through the land.
However, the telegraph was one up
on the train, because it was faster!
From the 1850s, late trains, accidents
and traffic could be communicated
reliably on the rail system,
both in the US and Britain.

### Did You Know?
Today, high speed
Internet cables
are also laid along
existing tracks,
borrowing the
railroads'
'right of way'.

## A Single Pulse

The telegraph message, or telegram, crosses continents in the 1850s. An American merchant seeks the help of the British and American navies to lay a well-insulated telegraph cable across the floor of the Atlantic Ocean. The cable stretches 3,200 km (2,000 mi) and goes 3 km (2 mi) deep. On 16 August 1858, President James Buchanan and Queen Victoria exchange messages on this line.

THE WHITE HOUSE
Telegraph Office

Is that message from Buckingham Palace still coming in??? It's been 8 DAYS already!

It's only half done... and so far, it's only Queen Victoria listing her various titles...

## Truncated Talking

Telegrams are charged per word, and this transforms the way language is used in them.

- In 1958, Lee Kuan Yew (Singapore's first prime minister) is craving a steam boat dinner. He writes ARRIVING TODAY BATTLESHIP to save on spending on more words. Alas, no steam boat for dinner!

- There are no more social greetings like DEAR and YOURS TRULY, nor are there any expensive adjectives and pronouns.

- The shortest telegram is said to have been sent by Oscar Wilde to his publisher about his new book. It reads "?" And the reply is "!"

- In April 1912, a heartbreaking telegram reads: SOS SOS CQD CQD TITANIC. WE ARE SINKING FAST. PASSENGERS ARE BEING PUT INTO BOATS. TITANIC.

## The Talking Telegraph

The telegraph lays the groundwork for the next big step. Alexander Graham Bell develops a new technology that uses electric currents to send sound (instead of Morse code) through the wire.
At first, he calls it a "talking telegraph".
Although there are a few scientists working on similar ones at that time, Bell is the first to patent the telephone in 1876.

Alexander Graham Bell

<Electronic Voice>
Hello. This is the Port Customs Authority. There is a parcel addressed to you that contains illegal goods, and you will be prosecuted for it. To avoid the fine, please press "3", followed by your credit card number...

## Gone Wireless

By the late 19th century, Italian inventor Guglielmo Marconi has extended this technology to a radiotelegraph, which sends the Morse code signal wirelessly. This is the basis for all radio (and Wi-Fi) networks now, and in 1912, the only reason it is possible for the Titanic to send distress signals at sea, saving 700 lives.

Answer: A Sign for Change

# WILD WILD WEB

The invention of the Internet blasts open
an information superhighway we now live on.
It completely changes the way life is lived, especially
with the discovery of the World Wide Web.

## Cold War Weapon

In October 1957, the Soviet Union launches Sputnik, the
world's first satellite, into space. On the other side of
the **Cold War**, the Americans sit up in alarm. They are
particularly concerned that if the Soviets attacked, just
one missile might destroy the entire telephone network.

### What's That?

The **Cold War** developed
after World War II, between
the two superpowers then,
the US and the Soviet Union.
It ended in 1991, with the
collapse of the Soviet Union.

### Did You Know?

The term Cold War is first used
by English writer George Orwell
in 1945, to refer to a nuclear
standoff between "monstrous"
superpowers with weapons to
wipe out millions of people.

## Hot Potato Routing!

In the 1960s, American engineer Paul Baran comes up with a solution for a network to survive a nuclear attack. It does not depend on one central system nor does it run on one fixed line. It works instead by bouncing off any **node** in a computer network (like a hot potato), until it reaches its destination.

### What's That?

A **node** is a point on a network of computers. The Internet works by transmitting information (or data) from one node to the next. If one node was slow or faulty, the block of data would just jump to another.

### Did You Know?

This is also the way the brain works: it does not rely on a single set of cells to do a certain function. It is able to bypass a node that doesn't work and use another one. This is what convinces Baran he could do the same with communications.

## Pack It Up and Send It On!

Baran creates "**packet switching**", which breaks data down into 'blocks' or 'packets'. These packets are much easier to transmit in smaller pieces and do not have to take a specific route, just the fastest one. They then reassemble at the destination computer as a message or file.

**Did You Know?**
"Packet switching", now a universal term in computing, came from Donald Davies (the UK) who was developing the same idea at that time.

## Bits and Bytes

The way the telegraph works (sending coded messages in dashes and dots) is similar to the Internet. Data travels in bits, or binary code, which is a mathematical system using 1s and 0s.

- A byte is a chunk of eight bits.
- Each letter on the keyboard is one byte, made up of a series of 1s and 0s.
- Computers read and interpret all text, images and sound in binary, so HELLO is: 01001000 01100101 01101100 01101100 01101111.

34

## Lo and Behold

In late 1969, a professor and his students at the University of California, Los Angeles, send the first packet-switched message to another network computer 480 km (300 mi) away at Stanford University. It only reads "LO", as the UCLA student is about to type "LOGIN" into the Stanford computer when it crashes.

Professor? I'm not sure if those guys at UCLA are taking this experiment seriously enough...

>LOL

## A Virtual Postal Service

In the 1970s, computer scientists Bob Kahn and Vint Cerf propose a standard 'digital envelope' tagged to each packet that can be read by any computer or network. Called **TCP/IP** (Transmission Control Protocol/Internet Protocol), this enables an IP address to be read by any **Internet**-connected device, and sent along, until it reaches its destination.

## Forgettable and Forgotten

ARPANET employee Ray Tomlinson sends the first email in 1971. He is also the man behind the user @ host email format. Looking on his keyboard for a letter that would never be found in a username or file, he chooses "@". Tomlinson sends this first email in the world to himself, to a computer next to his. Like all test messages, it is forgettable and definitely, forgotten.

He may have also invented spam email... :P

## Enquire Within Upon Everything

At CERN (the European Organisation for Nuclear Research) in Geneva, Switzerland in 1980, 25-year-old British computer scientist Tim Berners-Lee has had enough of moving to separate computers to access different sets of data. To make life easier for himself, he uses a database system called hypertext, to connect easily to all his files. He calls it Enquire, after the title of a book he read as a child.

**Did You Know?**

As a teenager at Oxford University, UK, Berners-Lee built his own computer using an old television set.

## Neither TIM nor MOI

By the end of the decade, Berners-Lee has coded a common Hypertext Transfer Protocol (HTTP) for the Internet. It enables researchers like him to share files for review any time, anywhere in the world.

He tosses up a few possible names for this:

- The Information Mine (or TIM, his first name).
- Mine of Information (or MOI, meaning "me" in French).
- Information Mesh, which sounded too much like "mess".
- The World Wide Web, which gives the right sense of a global map "allowing anything to link to anything".

38

## Free and Unfettered

Kahn, Cerf and Berners-Lee gave up their inventions for free. By doing this, they ensured that their protocols (TCP/IP and HTTP) were used by everyone, making the Internet and World Wide Web as big as they are today. Thirty years later, Berners-Lee has said he is devastated by some of the effects of the Web (*see page 51*).

### Did You Know?

For his contributions to the World Wide Web, Berners-Lee is knighted by Queen Elizabeth and made Knight Commander, the second highest honour in the Order of the British Empire (OBE).

# THE SOCIAL MEDIA SPIRAL

Moving closer to the 2000s, advances to the Internet and World Wide Web make it much easier to connect, keep up with the news, and be entertained. Like a whirlwind, the rise of social media makes life so much simpler but also more complex.

*Only 100 users, Jarkko?*

*Yeah, I don't think that many people would really be interested in it.*

## Chat Crosses Continents

In 1988, before WhatsApp and WeChat, 21-year-old Finnish student Jarkko Oikarinen creates the Internet Relay Chat (IRC). It allows users to connect to other **servers** and chat with people outside their network. Initially planned for 100 users, IRC goes global.

### What's That?

A **server** is a computer that runs the functions for all the workstations (called "clients") in a network.

### Did You Know?

When the Gulf War breaks out in the early 1990s, radio and television broadcasts in Kuwait are cut. But many people are still able to access news from the front line through IRC.

40

## From Garage to Google

In the mid 1990s, there are about 10 million documents on the World Wide Web. Stanford PhD students Larry Page and Sergey Brin decide to organise these better, by ranking a web page through the number of 'back links' made to it from other sites. They call it BackRub! The duo work from their room, using Lego bricks to hold the huge storage hard drives, and sometimes crashing the university network.

Hi Sergey, lots of us are aching from sitting too long at our desks... and we heard that you and Larry were giving back rubs?

I'm here for the Lego...

Isn't she a bit young for university?

Child prodigy...

## Check That Spellcheck

I thought it was GOOGLE because I was becoming google-eyed staring at the screen!

By late 1997, BackRub becomes Google, which is a typo by one of the founders' friends, who was trying to see if the domain name was available. It was meant to be Googol, which is the digit 1 followed by 100 zeroes, to reflect the massive amount of information it organises.

41

## Programming Prodigy

At age 12, Mark Zuckerberg is tired of running up and down the stairs at home. He programmes his own instant chat system (Zucknet) to relieve those tired little legs! In high school, he writes Synapse, a programme that learns the user's taste in music, and recommends playlists.

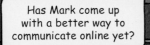

### Hot or Not

Fresh at Harvard University, Zuckerberg creates Facemash "just for fun". It allows his college mates to rate the looks of students on campus. Facemash goes so viral, it crashes part of the school's network. Zuckerberg gets in trouble for using photos without permission (on a school network). In early 2004, he starts www.thefacebook.com.

# Technology to the Rescue

Over time, the development of the (1) personal computer and the (2) supercomputer (allowing data to be stored and sent at high speeds) enables the Internet and Web to become what it is today. Finally, the (3) mobile phone skyrockets **social media** into a major way of life.

## Wardrobe Malfunction

At the 2004 Super Bowl 'live' performance in the US, Justin Timberlake pulls off fellow singer Janet Jackson's outfit and exposes part of her chest for a split second. Timberlake apologises for the "wardrobe malfunction", a phrase that is now in the dictionary. At that time, "Janet Jackson" enters the *Guinness World Records* as the "most searched" in Internet history.

## Me at the Zoo

In 2005, 26-year-old Jawed Karim is frustrated that he cannot find footage online of this malfunction fiasco. At the same time, his colleagues at then-startup company, Paypal, are having trouble sharing the video of a dinner party through email. Thus, the birth of YouTube. The first ever YouTube video is "Me at the zoo" by Karim.

### Did You Know?

As of 2020, Google founders Page and Brin still have main control over Alphabet, which owns companies literally from A-Z including Google, Waze and YouTube.

# A MUSHROOM CLOUD

With the railroad, as with the Internet —
these change makers to communications start with
so much promise, but come with unexpected effects.

## What's That?

A **mushroom cloud** refers to a mushroom-shaped cloud after a huge explosion, but is used here to refer to the effects of technology.

PRETTY BUBBLES

NOOooooo oo o

## Did You Know?

In the 2000s, the "dotcom bubble" bursts spectacularly. People hope to cash in on the next big killer app, but end up losing **trillions** of dollars. Only one in every two dotcom companies succeeds in the end.

## Burst That Bubble

When the novel concept of travelling by train begins to take off in Britain in the mid 1800s, many new railway companies jump on the bandwagon. This leads to what's called a "speculative bubble" where businesses and regular folks put money into these promising new companies hoping to get rich quick, but the companies end up failing.

## What's That?

A **trillion** is one million million, with 12 zeroes.

## Fifteen-Minute Fame

By the 2010s, social media and its ability to go viral is a double-edged sword. Brands engage on all sorts of tactics to fight for customers on a cluttered platform.

## Swipe That Hair

In 2017, an ingenious Chinese shoe company produces an ad with a strand of hair on its post, inducing annoyed users to swipe at the hair and unwittingly land on its website. The company is admired for its clever trick, but not so much the myopic marketing. Users are angered and the ad is removed.

46

## The Algorithm Attack

With so much new information daily, social media platforms use an **algorithm** to feed posts to users based on what they viewed or 'liked' in the past:

- A user, already biased towards a certain view, might see posts confirming this view. This could divide society even further, because other views do not get fed to the user.

- In the UK, a teenager looking at posts on depression had more such posts fed to her. Some governments are looking at laws to hold social media companies responsible for their content, especially to protect the young.

### What's That?

An **algorithm** is a set of steps performed by a computer programme to achieve a certain result. On social media, this goal is to keep users engaged for as long as possible.

## A Pivot to Privacy

In the 2010s, a Russian researcher runs a 'personality quiz' on Facebook, collecting **personal information** from users and their friends. This data was possibly used to create ads to influence voters in the 2016 US presidential election. Facebook comes under fire for not protecting tens of millions of its users.

Professor "Spectre"? I'm "Mister X" and this is "Mister Spooky" and "Mister Cuddles". We'd like to speak to you about online privacy and unauthorised collecting of information about us...

Uh-oh...

CAMBRIDGE ANALYTICS

ON THE INTERNET YOU ARE / AREN'T / CAN BE / CAN'T BE / SHOULD BE ANONYMOUS

## When Angry Won the Internet

The BBC (British Broadcasting Corporation) calls 2015 the year that angry won the Internet. It reports half a million racial slurs just on Twitter that year. One view is that social media has brought everything out to air, with Internet trolls using words to attack from behind an anonymous wall.

## What's That?

Phishing is another form of **social engineering**, a term used to mean conning a person to reveal sensitive information. It could come as a link in an email, leading the victim to click on it and type a password.

# A History of Hacking

At age 16, career hacker Kevin Mitnick does his first crack into a computer system and steals software. He is said to be a **social engineer**, using phone calls and email messages to persuade people to part with their passwords. Mitnick was one of the most notorious **black hat** hackers chased through the US by the FBI (Federal Bureau of Investigation). He is jailed in 1995, and when released in 2000, banned from using the Internet for a few years.

## Did You Know?

Mitnick makes the mistake of hacking into Tsutomu Shimomura's files in 1994 and distributing them online. Shimomura, a **white hat** hacker, does a back hack to Mitnick, leading to his arrest.

## What's That?

**White hat** hackers are 'ethical' hackers who use their ability for good. They are sometimes hired by companies to test how secure their systems are.

## The FOMO Factor

The 21st century sees a slew of studies on human behaviour as a result of socialising on the Internet.

- FOMO (Fear of Missing Out): An anxiety from not wanting to miss out on the latest.

- Internet addiction: A condition that exhibits brain patterns similar to those who are addicted to drugs.

- Popcorn brain: A state where the brain is so accustomed to pops of instant information that the attention span is shortened.

- Cyberbullying: The use of social media to spread rumours and hurtful images.

- Depression: The overuse of technology with less time spent on processing emotions.

### Did You Know?

Researchers also discover that "phantom vibrations" are a real thing. The brain is so used to expecting a ping on the phone, that the body even feels it.

## How the Web Was Lost

On the 30th anniversary of the World Wide Web in 2019, Berners-Lee writes an open letter to the world. He is devastated by the effects of his creation and says that the Web has made life easier on so many counts, but has also lost its way. He writes that if social media was going through adolescence in the early 2000s, it is now time for it to grow up.

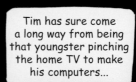

Tim has sure come a long way from being that youngster pinching the home TV to make his computers...

# OF SWEETS AND SIMPLE PLEASURES

The Internet has also warmed the hearts of many and united people in positive ways. It has had a major impact on culture, through the way an idea catches on and takes the world by storm.

## Meme the Gene

The word **meme** (meem) is coined by English author Richard Dawkins in 1976, in his book, *The Selfish Gene*. He calls it the 'cultural equivalent' of a gene, like a thought or style that passes from person to person, making changes in society. It has now come to mean an infectious idea that people relate to globally, that spreads on the Internet.

## Dancing Baby

In 1996, American Michael Girard
designs Baby Cha-Cha-Cha,
a 3D baby dancing in diapers.
It goes viral by email, before
landing on the World Wide Web.
By 1998, Dancing Baby appears
in an episode of US TV series,
*Ally McBeal*, sealing its fate as
one of the early memes to go viral.

### Did You Know?

The world's first
webcam image
was produced by
computer scientists at
Cambridge University,
UK in 1993. The image
was of their coffee pot.
And more importantly,
whether it was empty.

## #TheDress

In 2015, Scottish folk singer Caitlin McNeill breaks the Internet. She posts a photo of a £50 striped dress which she can't tell is (a) gold and white or (b) blue and black. This question lands strong responses on both sides. Clever marketing jumps in immediately:

- Dunkin' Donuts makes and posts a blue/black and a gold/white icing donut and says, "Doesn't matter... it still tastes delicious."

- Lego pulls out two figurines decked in the two sets of colours and quips, "We found a way around science! You can have both!"

For the record, the dress was blue and black.

## Sweeter, Together

A few days before the 2016 US election, ice cream brand Ben & Jerry's takes aim at the angry views that have divided the world. In a viral video, a lemon with a comb-over riles up his fellow lemons and says, "Zest is best." Peace comes to Coneville only when one lemon reaches out to a forward-thinking cherry who says, "We taste sweeter together!" Just the thing to amplify the message of unity and love — ice cream!

## Life is Beautiful

As of early 2020, China has 900 million Internet users, making it number one ahead of India, and then the US. A fair number enjoy live stream shopping, engaging with a seller 'live' on social media and buying on the spot. However, because the Internet reaches even the most rural areas, China and the world access gorgeous stories of humans:

- A farming couple in Wenzhou, Zhejiang fascinates millions with dance moves in the rice fields.

- A food delivery guy receives an unusual order: to pick up a few loaves of bread and feed the seagulls flying above a local dam.

GO AWAY... I DON'T HAVE ANY MORE BREAD

## From The Beatles to BTS

In 2020, a hundred million fans rallied to enter Korean band **BTS** into the *Guinness World Records*, making its latest music video, *Dynamite*, the most watched YouTube video in 24 hours. UK band The Beatles rocked the world, minus the Internet, in the 1960s. Forty years later, BTS is the only other group to sell more than 1 million albums in the US.

Billboard Hot 100

57

Online shopping

Trending Korean boy bands

Spreading fake news

Sharing unverified Internet stories

Cute cat videos

Looks like information spreading on the Internet may not be as effective as we think...

Our planet is in peril!

Greta Thunberg

Sir David Attenborough

## Rise Above the Noise

Not to be outdone by the young ones, 94-year-old David Attenborough creates an Instagram account that collects a million followers in 4 hours 44 minutes. In his first post, with a heartfelt video, he tells why he has come to the platform to save the world:

"Continents are on fire.
Glaciers are melting.
Coral reefs are dying.
Fish are disappearing
from our oceans.
The list goes on and on.
Saving our planet is now
a **communications challenge**."

### What's That?

A **communications challenge** refers to whether a message will successfully go through to its target audience.

# THE FINAL FRONTIER

The ARPANET in the 1960s was hosted on computers as big as a room. Now there is cloud storage, and we carry more processing power on a mobile phone in our pockets. Once the stuff of science fiction, high-tech gadgets from books and movies are not so far off from reality.

## Checkmate!

In the late 1940s, Alan Turing builds an algorithm called Turbochamp to think two moves ahead in chess. His early computer is so slow, Turing works out the math on paper! By 1996, Russian world chess champion Garry Kasparov has beaten Deep Blue, IBM's chess-playing computer. Deep Blue's **Artificial Intelligence (AI)** is able to assess 100 million different chess positions in one second, and defeats Kasparov the following year.

### What's That?
AI (Artificial Intelligence) refers to a computer or programme that is built to 'think' and respond like a human.

### Did You Know?
Turing is better known as the man who cracks the Germans' encrypted messages sent wirelessly in Morse. By listening in on their attack plans, Turing changes the course of World War II.

## A Googol Times Harder

The game of Go, or 围棋 (wéi qí), is a 4,000-year-old Chinese board game using black and white stones, which requires multiple layers of strategic thinking. For decades, Google's AlphaGo could only play at the amateur level.

- AlphaGo is pitted against humans, to understand how they play, and to learn how to play better.

- There are a 10 to the power of 170 possible moves, more than the number of known atoms in the universe (and more than a googol).

- In 2016, it beats Go legend, South Korean Lee Sedol, in a landmark game watched by 200 million people worldwide.

## Bob and Alice Bargain

At Facebook in 2017, chatbots Bob and Alice are instructed to negotiate with each other for balls, hats and books. The debate quickly breaks down as the robots appear to chant to each other in a strange, truncated English.

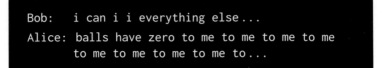

```
Bob:    i can i i everything else...
Alice: balls have zero to me to me to me to me
       to me to me to me to me to...
```

Facebook abandons the project, leading some to say the company was spooked. Facebook clarifies that their only interest is in "having bots who could talk to people."

## Putting Thoughts Into Action

In the early 2000s, a young American man, Matthew Nagle, is stabbed in an incident and paralysed from the neck down. A tiny chip (to read nerve signals) is implanted in his brain and connected to a cable outside. Nagle learns to 'think' thoughts to control a computer mouse. He changes TV channels, sends emails and plays "Pong" (like ping-pong) with his mind.

# I, Robot

BCI (Brain-Computer Interface) research uses the brain waves coming from neurons in the brain, as they spark from a particular thought. A computer then reads and organises these thoughts (such as "move mouse left/right") to translate them into action. In this first human experiment, Nagle soon learns to just imagine moving the mouse, rather than imagine his arm doing the work!

Matt Nagle 1979-2007

Powered by the MiND

## Mind to Machine Messaging

Elon Musk, the man behind space flight and electric cars sets up Neuralink in 2017. It is building a robot that is able to safely implant this tiny brain chip. The idea is that the mind can take in information much faster than it could push it out through the voice, or typing on a keyboard. This tech would allow the mind to talk directly to a machine.

## A Human Alien Language

The sound of neurons sparking and connecting in the brain has been described as a 'music' of static sounds. Musk predicts that in the future, people might not need to talk anymore. They might use this alien-like mind language to communicate. However, does this mean thinking criminal thoughts will make you one?

**Did You Know?**
Scientists say that the problem is interpreting brain signals — most of the function of the brain is still a mystery.

## Machine to Machine

The Internet of Things (IoT) refers to everyday objects connected to the Internet, which come together to make life easier:

- At home, the IoT could get your coffee machine cranking once you wake. A sensor in the fridge could send an order to the grocer when your milk expires.

- For a country, IoT could be used to manage water supply, or take care of the health of the elderly through wrist bands they wear.

Recently, the term the Internet of Everything (IoE) has come up, where the physical world merges with the digital world. And the Internet is invisible because it is everywhere.

### Did You Know?

Self-driving cars are being developed all over the world. In Shanghai, robotaxis have started plying the roads, with a human 'driver', just in case.

The phone was talking to me just now... Why haven't you called your grandmother this week?

You're drinking too much coffee!

Yeah... and stop snacking so much! You're putting on weight!

# MY FUTURE WORLD

Dear Reader,

You were born into a digital world. This book has barely touched the tip of the iceberg on the digital future you face. There is AR (Augmented Reality), space travel and much more we can't even imagine yet.

The pioneers in this book were young, like you. Here's your space to write about, or draw your future world!

Love,

&

# HWEE'S HANDBOOK TOOLKIT

The stories in this book converge onto how we communicate with each other today. One way of using this information is to study our past to map our future. Here are a few ideas to start your own journey:

## The Horseless Carriage of Doom!

When the railroads first started, naysayers approached these self-moving vehicles with fear. Was it black magic? Did it spell doom for humanity? In the same way, we look at the powerful influence of the Internet with some trepidation. We have the power to balance the good with the bad.

It's just not the same without the horse...

## Freedom of Mis Information

Information is free on the Internet, and so is fake news. Enter with a filter, and cross check new information against the news, or other stronger sources. People might also persuade you to a certain viewpoint with misinformation, so staying alert to this helps.

MISS ANTHROPY

MISS DIRECTION

MISS LEADING

MISS DEMEANOUR

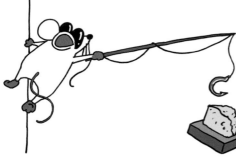

## Build A Better Mousetrap...

and the world will beat a path to your door. Google, for example, did not succeed because they were the first. They succeeded because they had the best idea and solution to the problem at hand.

## With Power Comes Responsibility

From Facebook to Tik Tok, social media platforms are well aware of the problems with their algorithms, even as they seek to create the best experience for users. If the algorithm might narrow our scope, then we open our minds, ask questions and seek information actively.

TAKE TOG
Tik Tok
Tick Tock
THiCK TALK

MORE THAN ONE VIEW...

# ACKNOWLEDGEMENTS

Lots of Thank Yous to:

Koon Goh, for his clarity of purpose and tech knowledge;

Lydia Leong, my editor, for volleying back drafts
as fast as I hit them at her!

And finally, communications academics, fellow
journalists and editors at news organisations
and especially at Britannica and History.com

# ABOUT
# HWEE AND DAVID

Trained at the Northwestern University Medill School of Journalism, former CNA (Channel NewsAsia) reporter and editor **Hwee Goh** put together this handbook from a few hundred sources online. Hwee lived through the development of the Internet, from text-based IRC at college, to building an HTTP web page as a young  adult. Hwee is now a media and editorial consultant. She continues to curate stories on @hweezbooks.

 Illustrator **David Liew** and Hwee were in junior college together studying strange but true moments in modern world history. David continued on to be a history teacher before becoming illustrator to many bestselling book series. David's art often takes on humorous angles appreciated by his fans, young and old. It is with this added layer of art, that the Change Makers team hopes to engage young readers on their own journey of discovery into this world's unknowns.